love and peace

coloring book

love and peace

coloring book

NINA TAYLOR

SIRIUS

SIRIUS

This edition published in 2022 by Sirius Publishing, a division of
Arcturus Publishing Limited,
26/27 Bickels Yard, 151–153 Bermondsey Street,
London SE1 3HA

Copyright © Arcturus Holdings Limited

ISBN: 978-1-3988-1857-6
CH006754NT
Supplier 34, Date 0122, Print run 001

Printed in the Czech Republic

Introduction

Get ready to celebrate peace and love with this beautiful coloring book by Nina Taylor. Her original artwork of birds, butterflies, sunsets, hearts, and flowers invites you to dive into a gentle world of romance and reverie.

The *Love and Peace Coloring Book* will help you to chill out and unwind. The detailed outlines in these pages are custom-made for coloring in any way you choose. While doing so you'll discover a quiet space where you can soothe your mind and focus on living in the present moment.

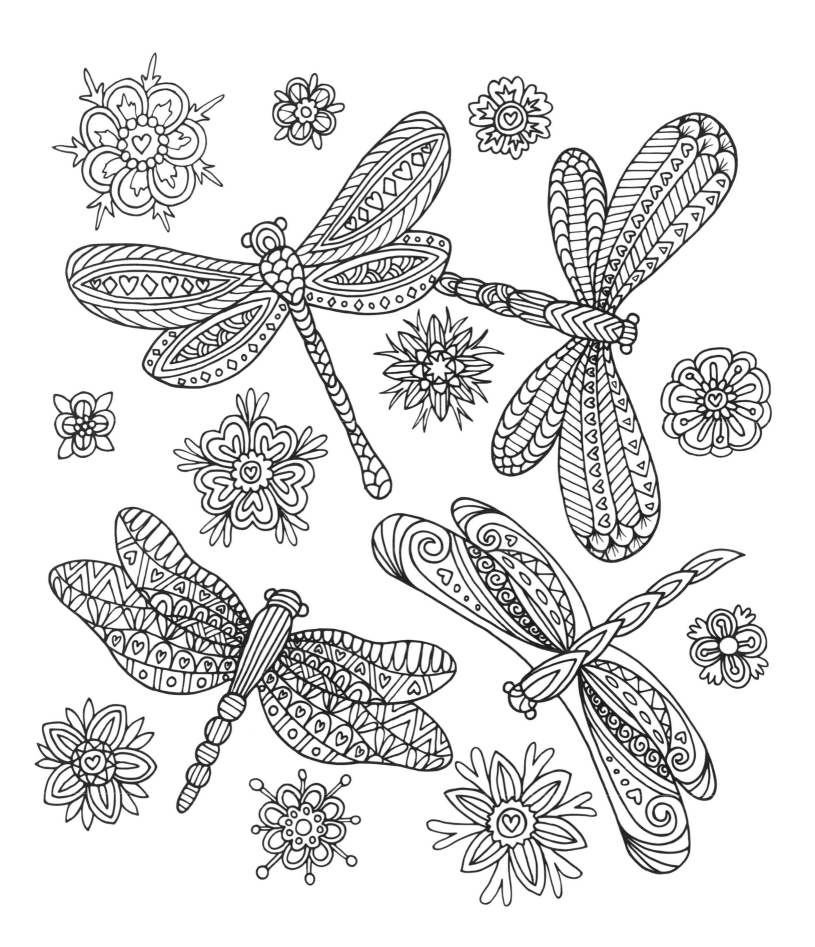